We Thought It Would Last Forever

Mary Frances Howard

We Thought It Would Last Forever

Copyright © 2018 by Mary Frances Howard

CenterPeace Publishing
www.centerpeacepublishing.com

Cover Painting – "Joe's Field" by Artist, Raney Rogers, long time friend.

ISBN 978-0-9861947-2-6

DEDICATED TO my children *Lee Lloyd (Renee)*
and Lisha Lueck (Joel), and grandchildren Seph, Elan,
Kristen and Caleb.

IN MEMORY OF *my beloved sister Margaret Baker.*

SPECIAL THANKS TO *Janet Kangas, without whom this*
book would never be.

"For I know the plans I have for you," declares the Lord, "plans to prosper
you and not harm you, plans to give you hope and a future." Jeremiah 29:11

CONTENTS

Foreward

Mary Frances Howard is known for her kind heart and compassionate ear. Some know her as Mary Frances, some as Frances and her brother calls her Murf (as a little boy he couldn't say Mary Frances). Whatever you call her, she always responds with kindness. The first time I met her we had agreed to meet at her home in Fuquay-Varina so that I could interview her for an article in the local newspaper. When I showed up, I had the worst cold that I had no business sharing with anyone. Frances welcomed me, sat me down and gave me tissues, couch drops and hot tea. We immediately became friends.

The story that I wrote then was about her work with the Alzheimer's Association. For many years, Frances led a support group for caregivers of those with Alzheimer's Disease in Fuquay-Varina, NC, after the death of her husband, Lester Howard. Frances wanted to help others who were experiencing the heartbreak of taking care of a family member suffering from an unforgiving illness. She learned the hard way how connected all of us are as we help each other through some tough times. When Lester became ill in the late 1990s, there wasn't much information available to help family members deal with the inevitable changes happening in their lives. Frances kept a journal and learned as much as she could so that she could find healing for herself and help others.

Her friends and family encouraged her for many years to write her own story. What she had experienced as she helped Lester through his seven-year journey with Alzheimer's was just part of the story. She had so much to share about the joys and sorrows in her own life, but there never seemed to be time to write about it. She asked God for the time to read and write. Right about then, Frances had two strokes that caused her to change her focus from helping others to rebuilding her own life. "God gave me plenty of time to read and write." To help her build the muscles in her right arm and hand, she was given the newspaper so that she could copy the words. Frances said, "why not write my own story?" and that's what she did.

We reached the very end of writing her book when Frances fell and broke her pelvis. Whatever the obstacle, she faces it head on. She recovered quickly and continues to focus on the gifts in her life.

It has been a joy to help her share her life on these pages.

Janet Kangas

Editor

The Early Years

I'm not sure where I was born on November 3, 1937. I always thought it was at the black house, an unpainted frame house, where Mama and Daddy lived when they were first married. Cousin Peggy Lindley said that Dr. McPherson delivered most of the grandchildren at Ma Mary's, which was in Teer, NC. The black house had three rooms – an add-on kitchen, a screened-in back porch and a front porch and an upstairs that was floored. In it was a big cedar box (probably built by Daddy who was a skilled carpenter who built our new white house when I was about 12 years old). The cedar box held our winter clothes and Christmas gifts from Santa Claus.

In the front room, called the living room because it had the sofa in it until a cat peed on it! – Sis Margaret and I slept in that room in a double bed. Bob and Berry slept in a twin bed. Don't know how! Bro Berry slept many nights at Dodie's, I guess. Dodie was our father's father.

We were happy there. We did not know we were "dirt poor". I was never hungry or cold and never had junk food. We did have a Pepsi on Sundays. Daddy stopped at Mr. Zan Crawford's store for gas for his commute to the Legget & Myers Tobacco factory where Chesterfield cigarettes were made. He always came out of the store with our one Pepsi. When we got home, Mama split the drink in four glasses. A knife was used to measure each one so that we could be sure that no one got an ounce more. Pepsi has never been so good as that one fourth.

There were four of us children. Berry Gene, named for our great-

1

grandpa Berry Andrews and our mama's daddy, Seymour Eugene Teer. I came next, Mary Frances, named after Grandma Mary Teer and Grandma Fannie Andrews. Two years later Margaret Faye was born. She was named after Mama's sister, Margaret Lewis. Brother Walter Robert (Bobby) was born 13 months after Sis Margaret. He was named after Mama's brother Walter.

Mama Ruth said the more children she had, the faster they came! Brother Bob had pneumonia when he was just a little fella. Mama was real concerned. I remember his crib had a sheet tent over it so steam from a kettle on a wood stove would help him breathe. He lives today!

Papa Gene came once a week so we could go to visit Ma Mary. When we went to school, he only came in the summer. Mama and Ma Mary would can green beans and corn and beet pickles. One time the pressure cooker exploded! Green beans and glass went all over the kitchen ceiling! By the grace of God, they were not hurt.
We were self-sufficient in our childhood years, in all areas, even in playing. A baseball thrown over the black house which had a tin roof was one of our games. One would throw the ball and yell, "Annie Over," then start running around the house to tag the catcher!
Sis Margaret and I would play hop scotch in lines drawn in the dirt near the front porch.

I always dreamed of having my own girl's bike. It never happened. One of the boys got a boys' bike (it was for all of us). When it came time for me to learn to ride one, Daddy showed me how to get on it and how to pedal. I do not remember him showing me how to stop! Anyhow, he got me all fixed and gently sent me down the driveway which was on a little hill. Away I went, but out of control. I did not fall off but I did wrap around the grapevine post which was at the bottom of the driveway! Got right up and did the next ride better.

We had two swings in one of the 100-year-old pear trees in front of the black house. The greatest freedom I ever knew was soaring as far as the ropes would go!! The man who ran the motor-grader which kept the dirt road, the main road, always ate his lunch under the other pear tree in the yard. We loved to pick on him. Mr. Wilbur Lloyd was his name.

Going to Church

Going to church, Antioch Baptist Church, was a BIG part of our family life. We got all dressed up to go to God's house. Daddy was made Sunday School Superintendent when I was about 10 years old. We had to be there on time to start at 10 a.m. on the dot. Before it started when the Spirit moved Mr. Gooch, I suppose. Mr. Gooch started everything late!

So, I had to play the piano for the opening song. I could play only two songs. I don't remember what they were. Speaking of Mr. and Mrs. Gooch being late for Sunday School, they were late for everything! They arrived when a bride and groom were leaving the church or when a funeral was over and the casket was being rolled down the aisle. They were seen walking to their barn after 10 at night.

Mrs. Mae Durham was one of our Sunday School teachers. Her class was the junior class. I guess the older class was the senior class.

Everybody had Miss Martha and Miss Mary Lloyd for Primary Class. They must have been saints. They never married, and neither did their brother Wallace. The three lived together in the family home.
Back to church. Not only did we go to Sunday School and preaching, we went back Sunday night for Baptist Training Union (BTU), and Wednesday night for GA (Girls' Auxiliary) and RA's (Royal Ambassadors) for the boys. Adults had Bible study. Women also had WMU (Women's Missionary Union). They met on Monday night in homes.

Vacation Bible School was held for a week every summer. We had

3

an assembly then went to classes. We had a break for snacks and Kool-Aid. We went home at noon.

Many life experiences came from our days in the Black House. We learned to live with what today seems bare. But, we had much – five houses - the Black house, a smoke house, a pump house, a chicken house and an outhouse.

In the smokehouse, hams and shoulders hung after they were cured – a process of keeping them in salt in a homemade wooden box.

The outhouse was our toilet. Instead of a commode, we had two holes cut out of a wooden bench. One was smaller for us children. It was a little hut with a tin roof and a door we could latch from the inside.

Wood was used for both heat and cooking. It was our job to keep the wood boxes filled – an every-day chore. I preferred taking in the cook stove wood. It was split from the big pieces used for the heater.

We learned hard work toting wood!

Monday was wash day. We had a wringer washing machine. It was in the screen porch along with two wash tubs on a rolling stand. Mama toted hot water from the cook stove and added cold water with a hose from the pump house. Clothes were sorted – whites first, colors, and last the denim jeans and overalls. After sending them through the wringer, the clothes were taken out to the clothesline and hung with wooden clothes pins. Bath cloths were hung on an old barbed wire fence. Sheets have never been the same since electric clothes dryers were invented!

Tuesdays were ironing days. Sheets and pillow cases were our "learning" pieces. Then we (Sis and I) got to iron jeans and overalls. Permanent press had not been invented yet! Overalls were jeans with a bib and straps over the shoulder. We girls wore feed- sack dresses. Chicken feed was delivered in sacks from the Farmers Exchange in Carrboro and we got to pick out the material for our dresses.

I learned life's lessons growing up on the farm. I never learned to milk a cow because I didn't want to go to the barn at 4:30 a.m. That applies to all things in life. If you don't know how to do it, you won't have to go to the barn.

I learned to value long-time friends. My friend Glenda Yow and I were friends since second grade. We're still friends 75 years later. Joyce Riley was another one. They lived in the Black House after we moved to the White House.

The Edmonds

A great day was when the Edmonds moved in to the farm house behind our house! Their truck was piled high with furniture and farm equipment. To our great joy there were children, lots of them. Hazel, Charlie, Addie Belle, Ruth Opal, Gertrude, Betty Jean, Billy, Mary, Linda, John and I don't know who else!

The younger ones were our play mates. John was brother Bob's. Mary was mine and Sis Margaret's. We had our own baseball team. And we girls jumped rope for a million miles!

Mr. Edmonds raised tobacco and sugar cane. We helped them put in tobacco. He also had a molasses mill. In the fall, they cut the cane in stalks which they then put in the grinding machine. It pushed out the syrup which was boiled down to make molasses. It was in the woods behind the Black House.

One day when we were "making molasses", I had to go to the toilet for #2. Mary and I went into the woods to take care of my "business". We had no toilet paper so Mary got some leaves for me to wipe with. Unfortunately, the leaves were poison oak! I became infected with a horrible full-body rash. Every part of my body itched!

I was bed ridden, with my hands tied to keep me from scratching! A doctor came every day to give me a shot. One day, Mrs. Edmonds was sitting with me when she told Mama I was scratching with my toes! Mama tied my feet! I got so mad at her!

Mrs. Edmonds twice snitched on me. The other time was when brother Berry and I went to visit them when they had the mumps. Mama and Daddy had not had them. Well, we saw Mama coming up the road, so we hid in the closet. But Mrs. Edmonds told Mama we were in the closet! Twice she did that.

We were switched all the way home to the black house. Berry got a switch, then me, on every step. We ended our missionary trips!

The Beach Trip

Ready for the beach! In back are Berry and Frances. Bob and Margaret are in front. (about 1949)

Mama and Daddy took us to the beach for the first time when I was about 10 years old. It was a big deal. I think it was Carolina Beach. Uncle Walter Teer, Mama's brother, had rented a house and was already there with Aunt Virgin and Pat. Don't remember if Bill was born yet.

All of us piled into the Ford and headed out. When we got to the beach, Daddy drove us to where we could see the ocean. What a sight! The water went to forever, it seemed. He told us we could see England just over the horizon. It seemed like it took all day to get there. When we got close, the sand was white. Daddy told us it was salt and the ocean was salty. We probably tasted the sand!

We all had bathing suits. Mama had a Catalina one. Daddy took her picture in it. She stood out beside the forsythia bush at the black house. He took a picture of us four beside the Ford car.

Oh! I forgot! Sis Margaret stepped on a mole trap and had a terrible puncture hole in her foot. Mama cried. Daddy said the salt water in the ocean would cure it and it did!

The Willow Tree

When we lived in the Black House there was a willow tree in the back yard. I watched it grow from a sapling to a huge tree. We had a sand box under its drooping branches. We spent many happy days making frog houses. We covered our feet with the damp sand, patted it down and then slid out our feet, backing out of the "frog houses."

The willow tree was Mama's source for switches. Our punishment for "crimes" was being sent to get a branch from the willow tree. She never hit us, just scared us straight!

School

We went to White Cross School. There were four classrooms – two on each side with the auditorium and stage in the middle. In the back, there were two walkways into the auditorium and the classrooms. The west end classrooms were the first and second grades in one room and the third and fourth grades in the other room. On the stage end, the fifth and six grades were in one room and the seventh and eighth grades were in the other room.

On the walkways, there were the girls' and boys' bathrooms. The girls' restroom was on the right and the boys' room was on the left, facing the building. From the girls' side, we went in the first and second grade room. Miss Margaret Stanford taught both.

Between the two walkways was a huge sandbox where we played.

Also, the walkways were great for my "gang" taunting Susie Copeland. Susie did not like me, nor did I like her! We each had our gang. Shirley Crawford had a hard time choosing who to join. Our gangs met on the walkways, Susie's on the boys' side, mine on the girls'.

Back to the school. We had a library behind the stage and the two classrooms where we learned about the world. I think I read all the books in it. The globe of the world was in there, also. My greatest claim I have from those days is beating Gordan (Cubby) Abernathy in the school spelling bee. I got to ride with the principal, Miss Mattox, to the county spelling bee in Hillsboro, NC. I lost when I wrote and "e" and not an "i" for "inquiries."

Back to the school building. We had a baseball field for the boys and a different one for us girls. There was a basketball "court," two goals set up beside the baseball field.

Old Friends – from left, Richard Andrews, Susie Copeland, Peggy Jean Riggins, Glenda Yow and Robert Lee Lloyd, my future husband.

Once, we girls were allowed to wear shorts at recess. I was so excited! Surely, R.L. Lloyd would notice me now! Well! He did! He said, "look at those bird legs!" I was crushed! The nickname"birdlegs" stayed with me for years. But, I did marry R.L.!

My one chance at stardom came on the stage at White Cross School. But, I was too sick to be in the play. I think Ruth Rogers took my place.

Ruth could hit a softball! Once, when I was running from first base to second base, Ruth hit a ball that came straight at my head. I have a hole over my left eye to this day.

Miss Stanford was the teacher in the first and second grades. She taught both grades! And, we did not have an aide. We learned to read, "Run Spot", and about "Dick and Jane." We had spelling and arithmetic. We had recess in the morning and the afternoon. Jump rope was the main girls game – also, dodge ball and hopscotch. There were only about 10, if that many, of us.

When I got to the third grade, I would do the work of the fourth grade, too! Miss Cates had Mama and Daddy come to her house to talk about me "skipping grade three," and I did! That made me the youngest in the class.

The students were me, Ruth Rogers, Glenda Yow and Bernice Ward. The boys were Larry Durham, Sam Lloyd, Alfred Zackery, David Mann and Hooker Butler. Occasionally, others would pass through. The Thorntons – Patricia was in our grade. She was not of our tribe! We were all poor, but the Thorntons were poor and rough. Charles Riley was also an outsider. Rumor had it that his mama was Indian and had no husband. He had the blackest hair I've ever seen. But, his brother Darrell did not!

I made straight A's until I discovered boys.

Main Events

Homecoming at Antioch Baptist Church surely was the biggest of them all! It is always on the second Sunday of August. There was a cemetery clean-up day the weekend before. The grounds got cleaned up, too. Tables, long ones, were placed under the huge, old oak tree near the cemetery. It was known as Second Sunday. Everyone who had attended church came "back home."

Mama and Grandma Fannie made me and Margaret new dresses. I don't know if the boys got new clothes. Mama and G. Fannie started cooking mid-week – pound cakes and always an angel food cake. The white icing always failed! Ham biscuits and fried chicken, fresh garden vegetables and chocolate pies filled their baskets and our stomachs. Those long tables were filled to overflowing. Former preachers were invited back to bring the message. There was special music, too.

Hog killing came in the winter, usually before Christmas. The weather had to be cold so the meat would not spoil. The pigs ate our table scraps, which were kept in a slop bucket under the kitchen sink. The pigs were our first garbage disposals! We had to lug the nasty bucket to the pig pen every day, rain, sleet or snow! A few cups of grain were added to the slop bucket.

When it was time to kill the hogs, neighbors came to help. Someone who was a good shot used a rifle to shoot the pigs between their eyes. Then, someone cut their throats to bleed them out. They were put in a vat of boiling water and the hair was scraped off with sharp knives or razor blades. The pigs were hung by their hind feet on a cross bar where they were cut open from tail to head, and the intestines and organs were removed.

The liver was used to make liver pudding. Tenderloins were cut out and sausage was ground up. Maybe the shoulders were used for that. The sausage was stuffed into bags that Grandma Fannie had made, or little patties were canned. All parts of the hog were used and we had meat and lard for a year.

Other Happenings

Twice a year – fall and spring – we went to Durham to get shoes. Sunday shoes and school shoes.

Back in my childhood, we fed the preacher on Sunday. It was our turn, and we had cleaned and cooked all week for the preacher and a visiting missionary to come to lunch. All was fine until I opened the closet in the dining room! We, Sis and I, had cleaned up and packed the closet full. We leaned on the door to put the latch on it. Well, Brother Bob needed his ball glove, so he opened the door, and everything tumbled out in front of the preacher and the missionary! I thought Daddy would wring my neck. The visitors laughed and said it looked like Fibber McGhee and Molly's closet. I thought I would die, but did not.

Mama Ruth and Daddy James

Emma Ruth Teer and
James Berry Andrews

To describe them, Mama Ruth was a butterfly, light and pretty. She made all around her better with her calm, quiet ways. She never hurried or got flustered. Daddy James was a bumble bee, zipping around getting things done! Always buzzing. That never bothered the butterfly. She knew to stop to smell the roses. She always said the turtle won the race!

We would be in the car, waiting for her to come out. In all fairness to her, she had gotten all four of us ready. She braided Margaret's and my hair from front to back.
Daddy could build anything. He worked

11

at Liggett and Myers Tobacco Company in Durham, making Chesterfield cigarettes. He brought home the loose ones that fell off the conveyor belt. Granddaddy Dodie smoked them. Met too! I would sneak one and go to their outhouse to smoke it.

Daddy had riders who he picked up every morning, no matter the weather. Even snow did not stop him! Once, the snow had drifted up to the kitchen window and he still went to work. His riders were Johnny Pearson, who was very fat; his sister, Hattie Mae, a Blackwood man, and Carl Andrews, who lived in Carrboro (no kin to us).

Mama's name was Emma Ruth Teer. Once, she burned the bread and Daddy said, "Did you burn the bread, my dear Emmie?" It was one of the few times she ever got mad!

Daddy was James Berry Andrews. They were poor and Democrats and Baptist! Mama's family were Republicans and Presbyterian. Her folks did not want her to marry Daddy, but my parents had a deep love that carried them through having four children, his brain cancer and many life trials.

Tobacco Time

Daddy raised 10 acres of tobacco just to keep us busy! The tobacco barn was where Uncle Berry's now sits. It had two flues running through it to cure the tobacco. Someone had to sleep under the shed on a cot. They had to keep the fires going in the flues. They were hot! The heat caused the green leaves to dry out – cured.
Then, the dried leaves were moved to a "pack house" where Dodie and others made a handful of leaves into a "hand" by wrapping a leaf around the top of the bundle. It took weeks to get ready for market where the cigarette companies bid on a big pile. Market was a big deal.

But, I got ahead of my story. I have to tell about growing tobacco.

Tobacco Raising

We learned hard, tedious work in the tobacco field. We had about 10 acres. Rows were laid by and tobacco seedlings were put in by hand. Dodie walked along, pushing a hand-held planter into the ground. It had a tank of water in it and a funnel where I walked along to drop the seedlings in. He pulled the lever to release the plant and water into the row. A tap of his toe set the plant. Over and over, we did that all day.

As the plants grew, we had to hand drop fertilizer. Then, when the plants grew they had flowers on top which we had to break off. That is called topping the tobacco. That made "suckers" at every leaf. They were removed by hand. This was called suckering. We also had to remove the tobacco worms and stomp on them. Berry and Bob would bite the worm's head off for spite or 50 cents!

Barning Tobacco

When the tobacco was ripe, the leaves were pulled off (called primed), starting with the bottom leaves. As the next row ripened they were primed, usually once a week. The leaves were piled into a tobacco sled which was pulled by a mule, usually named Nellie or Kate. The mule answered to "giddy up," "whoa," "gee" (go left), or "hah" (go right).

The sled was brought to the barn or the end of the field. At the barn, the tobacco was moved to a table where it was put on a stick by one of us – me, usually. I used tobacco twine to tie a "hand" on the stick. People called "handers" gathered the leaves into small bundles, keeping the tops even. These were quickly handed to the "looper" who wrapped the tobacco on each side of the tobacco stick until it was full. Then, the stick was placed in a pile. At the end of the day, we loaded up the sticks and took them to the tobacco barn. Men or boys (brothers Berry and Bob and neighbors) were the hangers. There were long poles that went from front to back on each side, and from head high to the top. Each pole was head high from the lower one and about 4-5 feet apart. The hangers stood sprattle-legged on the poles. The sticks were handed up to them end-to-end. When the barn was filled, the flues were fired up.

This was repeated every week in late summer. School did not start until tobacco season ended.

Me, Margaret and our brothers hired out to Howard Smith, Tom Bradshaw and the Rileys. Primers and loopers got five dollars a day. Handers got three. I learned to loop so I could make more money. Wherever we worked, lunch was provided. Wanda Smith was the best cook. Laura Bradshaw was the most fun.

New House

Mama and Daddy built a new house in 1950. She inherited money from Papa Gene Teer to pay for it. Daddy had a builder help put up the framing. A basement was put in first. We were so excited! We would have our own bedroom upstairs. The girls room was painted pink. The boys room was blue. The house was painted white, so we moved from the black house to the white house!

All of us worked on the house, nailing walls for plaster, putting down hardwood. Carpet was unheard of when we were growing up. Floors had linoleum on them. It came in sheets with floral designs on them. When we moved to the new house, we had hardwood floors except the kitchen. We had laid the floors ourselves. Someone came and refinished them. About once a year, me and Margaret had to rub paste wax on the floors. We used a sock which had been filled with the wax. Then when it dried, we polished them by sliding on them with old socks or soft rags. It was hard work.

The new house was wonderful. To have a bathroom was a dream. Dodie and Grandma Fannie lived right behind us so I visited many times a day. They were never busy, or so it seemed. Grandma Fannie did make butter once a week. She had a swinging wooden churn. It held five gallons of milk which had soured. I pushed that swing churn for many an hour.

The new house had an oil furnace. No more chopping, stacking or toting wood! We had a full basement where there was a wood cook stove, the washing machine and tubs. Later on, Daddy bought a freezer. Berry and Bob roller skated down there. I tried it once but wrapped around a post! Just like when I was learning to ride a bike! I did not do well with posts!

It was while we lived in the new house that I grew up. Every Saturday was housecleaning day – bathroom cleaned, floors dust mopped and kitchen floor wet mopped. Sheets were changed (washed on Monday). Sunday was church day and lunch at Grand Mary's, then supper at Grandma Fannie's. Always, there was fried chicken at both houses, and fresh vegetables in the summer and canned ones in the winter. There were home-made biscuits. Grand Mary made yeast rolls.

Both places were under huge oak trees which were very old. At Ma Mary's the men sat under the trees and we played in the yard which had a neatly trimmed hedge around one side and the front. There was a swing and rocking chairs on the front porch (as I have here at my house!).

Back to my grandparents.

Pictured from left are Fannie's brother Robert Smith and his wife Alice, and Grandpa Dodie and Grandma Fannie.

15

Ma Mary and Papa Gene's children were Charlie, Walter, Ruth, Tom, twins Gaston and Carrie, Seymour and Margaret.

Uncle Charlie Teer's children were Lemuel, William, Lydia, Thomas, Raney and Stanford. Uncle Walter had two children, Pat and Bill.

Ruth had Berry, Bob, Mary Frances and Margaret. Tom married late in life and his wife had one daughter, Juanita.

Gaston was married several times. In the U.S., he married Susie, who had one son, Harold. He abandoned her and told her he was going to Hawaii. He stopped in California long enough to marry and have twins. He married a woman named Alice. The twins were named Ruth and Marian. He joined the Navy and was stationed in Hawaii. He married a Japanese woman named Doris in Hawaii in 1942. They had three children, Seymour, Thomas and Lena.

Grand Mary and Papa Gene

Carrie had two sons, James and Charles. Her husband was Jim Snipes. Margaret was married to Jim Lewis. They had five children, Peggy, Carolyn, William, Helen Jean and Jimmy, who came late in

16

Margaret's life. William had polio when he was a toddler. He was in an iron lung at a hospital near Charlotte. When he got better, he came to Ma Mary's to live. So, she raised him. He learned to drive a tractor and worked on the farm. Seymour never married. He was killed when his plane crashed into a mountain in France during World War II, where he served in the U.S. Air Force. His remains were sent home about a year later to be buried in the Teer family plot at Bethlehem Church in Alamance County.

Grandpa Dodie and Grandma Fannie were my father's parents. William Reldue Andrews (called Dodie because his brother couldn't say his name) and Fannie Smith had three girls who died in infancy, Helen, Hilda and Nellie Fay. They had three boys, James Berry, Clyde and Exie Andrews.

Ma Mary had not only us, but other families for Sunday lunch sometimes – Aunt Margaret Lewis family - Peggy, Carolyn, Helen Jean and William and Jimmy (who came late). Uncle Walter came occasionally.

We would have Sunday supper at Grandma Fannie's. We had leftovers from lunch every Sunday. Clyde and Exie's families had lunch, then our family would come for supper. We caught lightning bugs in a glass jar after supper.

Frances' great-great-grandmother, Grandad Dodie's grandmother.

Both my grandparents had dairy farms. Dodie's was very small, but Papa Gene's was a big operation. Papa was also the mail carrier. His daddy had the post office, so the area was called Teer, NC. It is still on some maps.

There was a grape vine across the road on the "mountain" (which was really a big hill). When the grapes were ripe we climbed the mountain to eat them. There was also a dirt pile across from the house. We were told that there was a sack of gold hidden over there. We spent Sundays looking for that sack. Now we know they told us grandchildren that just to keep us out of their hair!

Teer Post Office was also a grain mill. Folks bought the grain to be ground into flour. There was a dam of water that was used to run the mill. We called it the mill pond. It was the neighborhood swimming hole until a pond was dug in the pasture between Papa's and Uncle Charlie's houses.

Aunt Janie was my favorite aunt. She was married to Daddy James' youngest brother, Exie.

Daddy's other brother was Clyde (the middle one). He married Fannie Mae who was from Carrboro. She was extremely frugal – tight, one could say. They built a big brick home and paid cash for it. They had two daughters, Janis and Bonnie.

I remember Aunt Janie and me and Mama Ruth going across the field in front of the white house. We were going to pick blackberries. Aunt Janie would sing for us Negro Spirituals like "Swing Low Sweet Chariot."

Teer Pond

Papa Gene had a farm pond dug for the cows. It soon became the neighborhood pool! The older grandchildren built a pier. It had a tower that Berry, Bob and other boys dived from. Every Sunday we could not wait to go down to the pond, but the rule was to wait an hour after eating to swim.

I learned to swim after someone pushed me off the end of the pier. I never could swim good, nor did I like it! Brother Berry could swim across the pond under water.

The cows were in the water at the far end where the spring that fed the pond was located. We never thought they were polluting the water when they pooped and peed in it! Life had not been ruled by the EPA and should not be now!

Granddaddy Dodie had a creek running through the pasture. We (Berry, Bob, me and Margaret) made a dam so we could have a swimming hole. That worked great until I made water wings out of the glass gallon jugs tied together by string. The idea was for me to lie down on the string on my chest. It worked good for a few seconds until the jugs hit together over my back. When that happened, they broke and shattered into our wonderful swimming hole.

That ended my inventing things.

I fell backwards into a cactus bush at Grandma Fannie's when I was about 8 years old! Uncle Exie pulled the thorns out of my rear end while I lay across Mama's knees. I never went near that bush again! Granddaddy Dodie had a chicken house where they raised them so the eggs could be sold. The baby chicks were delivered by mail until Abby Laura Lloyd started a hatchery and began selling chicks. She dyed some in Easter colors at Easter. We had one for a pet. It came in and out of the house, which really upset Mama. No animals were allowed in the house! Not even cats!

One day, Bitty got smoushed by a screen door closing on it! That ended Mama's problem. We had a funeral for Bitty at the edge of the field.

Papa Gene's Helper

June was a black man who worked on the Teer dairy farm. We loved him. I always thought he was the last slave. Papa Gene was

19

rumored to have had slaves – at least his family had them. June slept in a little room in one of the buildings. It had a single bed or a cot, a stove and a table. June entertained us by taking hot coals from the fireplace and holding them in his hand. He would toss them around, so he would not get burned.

June ate his meals on the screened side porch. What a treat to get to eat with him! I do not remember him joining the men under the tree after Sunday dinner. We had dinner at noon and supper at night.

June's last name was Baldwin. He moved to Aunt Margaret Lewis' farm to help her after her husband died during a snow storm. They had a dairy farm, too. Interesting – Aunt Carrie married a dairy farmer and Mama Ruth did also.

The Snipes' farm was bigger, as was Aunt Margaret's, which she ran after Uncle Jim Lewis died. Strange – all three Teer daughters married dairy farmers!

Snipes', Andrews', Teers' and Lewis' farms were operated by second generations – Berry Andrews, Charles and James Snipes, and William Lewis whose son Randy, still runs it. The Andrews and Snipes farms are no longer operating. Sarah Teer, great-granddaughter of Gene Teer, still runs the Teer farm.

June played the banjo and was very wealthy. He had saved all of his money. He took care of Aunt Margaret. He was so kind. Aunt Margaret's oldest son was paralyzed from the waist down. He had polio as a little boy. June came in the house every morning to bathe William and put his braces, shoes and clothes on him. He lived in a little house there on the farm and helped Peggy raise her children. We all learned compassion for the handicapped from June who cared for William.

Memories of Dodie and Fanny

Dodie's and Fanny's washing eggs to crate for Daddy to take to Durham to sell (reminded of this when I held an egg to put on to boil for breakfast). Their spartan life – yet contentment and simplicity ruled.

In their dining room was a sewing machine at the window. There was a chair lounge at the other end. A rocking chair for Fanny. What did Dodie sit in? The oil heater, an upgrade from wood. Linoleum floor covering, tiny refrig in the corner. Round dining table of oak. Side buffet – gold watch, a bed, a wardrobe, a trunk, a piano, a dresser, a bed, wicker love seat and chair. Light bulbs hung from the ceiling, worn rug for a carpet, fireplace in there. Side room – small bed, dresser and lamp. Back porch – milk separator, then milk cooler, milk cans and watermelon in that. Kitchen cabinet – and sink and stove. Then elec. Cupboard in the back with molasses and biscuits in it. What must it have been like to have only a Bible, a fire, a rocking chair and sewing machine, a few cows to milk every day; no TV, perhaps a radio and maybe a newspaper. How did they survive after Daddy was disabled?

Embarrassing Things I Did

Mama Ruth had a cousin who lived in New York and sang for the New York Met (Bill Kirkpatrick). He came to Hillsboro, NC, to sing in the Presbyterian Church. I don't remember his singing but I do remember that they passed a collection plate which I dropped on the hardwood floor! It had lots of coins in it, some of which rolled all the way to hit the altar. I could have gone through the floor!

When Mama and Daddy were building the new house, they worked at night on it. One night they drove up after dark and blew the horn for us to come and go with them to talk to someone to work on the new house. I was taking a sponge bath so just wrapped in a towel. I walked in front of the headlights in just a towel. Daddy was not happy! I was so embarrassed!

Summer Days

In the summer, we had a big garden from which green beans were canned. Potatoes were dug up (by plowing) and put in the dug-out cellar if not in the smoke house. Also, the canned vegetables were kept on shelves down there.

Canning was an all-day job. We canned at home or at Grand Mary's. Mama had a pressure cooker in which she put jars of green beans and watched the gauge at a certain temp for a set time. Once, the pressure cooker exploded. By the grace of God, neither she nor Grand Mary were hurt but green beans went everywhere, even on the ceiling.

We took corn and butterbeans (lima) to the neighborhood cannery. All the ladies sat around outside shelling beans or cutting off corn, which they then put in tin cans. These were put in a huge pressure cooker to be sealed.

Corn Shucking

Corn shucking was another big event. The corn stayed in the field until it was dry, then picked and brought to the barn and put in a big pile. When it was all pulled, the neighbors from far and wide gathered to shuck the corn. The men shucked and the women cooked a huge meal. That is where the phrase, "cooking for a corn shucking," came from. One time when Dodie was shucking fresh corn for freezing, he was giving the shucks to the bull and his knife went, too! I don't remember if he got it out or if it stayed in the bull!

When we got a food freezer, freezing corn was an all-day job. The men – Berry, Bob and others – picked a trailer load, which we all shucked, 100 or more ears! Then we pulled the silks off by brushing them with a firm bristle, after which it was time to put them in boiling water for a few minutes. Afterward, we cut the corn off the cob into dishpans which we held on our laps. One person would pack the corn in pint plastic bags to freeze. A good "mess" was 125 bags.

We had fresh corn all winter.

We also had chicken freezing day. The men killed the chickens and we put them in real hot water to make it easy to pull off the feathers. I never learned how to gut them. If you don't know how to do something, you will not have to go to the hen house or the barn to milk. I never learned, so did not have to get up at 4:30 a.m.

Courting

Growing up – time went fast as I grew up. My first date was a double date with Peggy Bowden and Tommy Rigsbee. (They later married.) Tommy had a Ford with a rumble seat (a sort of convertible). They picked me up at Granddaddy Dodie's. It was a blind date. We had never met. His name was Royce Tripp, but he was called Crammie Nose. He was a lineman on the Chapel Hill High School football team. My name became "Crammie" after that date! We went to a drive-in movie and I had no idea what to do so I just watched the movie. He never asked me out again!

My best friend was Joyce Riley. For a while, she lived in the black house with her parents and good-looking brother, Pete. We were together every day. Her mother, Mae, was terrified of storms. Every time one came up, I had to go over and sit with her even if Joyce or Pete were there! Joyce's father was Hoyt Riley and he had a job which made him be away all week.

Joyce and I had boyfriends who were from Durham. I don't know how we met them – probably at a square dance. Mickey Cotton was Joyce's boyfriend and Gerald Thacker was mine. They drove 1940 black souped-up Fords. They claimed to be hauling moonshine. They did not last long. We sat on the front porch. I don't remember that we went anywhere.

I dated three Lloyds. Jack Lloyd from Eli Whitney – he was related to Joyce and his dad courted Mama Ruth a few times. Then, I dated "Diz" (Larry Dean) Lloyd. He was also from Eli Whitney. Diz was a baseball pitcher, left handed, and very good.

Then, I realized my dream when I started dating Robert Lee Lloyd (R.L.). I had loved him from the time I was in fifth grade. He was very handsome. He, too, played baseball – second base.

R.L. quit school in the ninth grade so he could work to support his sister, Eleanor, when their mother died. She worked at the cotton mill In Carrboro. Their daddy was a hard man and did not work much. Mr. Green was a carpenter. He said he had heart trouble. And, sure enough, he did die of a heart attack during a snow/ice storm. He sat down from shoveling snow and died sitting up.

NC State Fair

The State Fair was a huge deal! It is in Raleigh at the fairgrounds in October. It celebrates farm life from milking to flowers. There were rides and entertainment. We had a square dance team called the White Cross Kittens. I was on the team, as was R.L. After one show, I had a date with Willie Baker who was R.L.'s best friend. Willie was wild! R.L. kept him out of trouble. While we were walking around, I wanted to ride the Tilt-a-whirl. Willie wouldn't ride, but R.L. did! As we were getting off, R.L. asked me to go to a movie Saturday night! I was thrilled. Well. Saturday night came, and he did not show up! I finally went to bed, broken hearted. I heard the phone ring and Mama answered it. The next morning, she told me that R.L. had a wreck on the way to see me. He saw me at the White Cross store later (I knew he was there when I saw his car from the bus from Chapel Hill High School that stopped up at the school). I couldn't wait to get to the store. He said we would try again come Saturday, and we did!

Susie Copeland

Susie Copeland was the "thorn" of my existence. We were enemies! Don't remember why. I think she was jealous of us because of our new house. Our feud involved half the girls of White Cross. We

24

each had our gang! We would stand on the walkway. Susie had the boys' restroom side and I had the girls' side. I remember quite well yelling at her unkind words. One time we got in a fight on the bus and I threw her shoe out the window. Rachel Thompson stopped the bus and made me get off and get it. Then I had to walk home! It was about a mile from Hwy 54 down Orange Grove Road. Many years later I saw her at a shower for her niece and asked her to forgive me. She was very cold but did say, "It was nothing." She was still hurt. But, some more years later I saw her again at a shower. I told her I was Born Again and was serious. She was very gracious in forgiving me. We were fighting because she was sitting beside Earl Land on the bus. He was my boyfriend!

Square Dancing

Square dancing was the main event on Saturday nights when I was young and even into my teen years and beyond. A group of men led by Garland Cates, who played the fiddle, made the music. My favorite was, and still is, "Orange Blossom Special." (I want it played at my funeral as I leave the church.) "Rocky Top," "Down Yonder," "and Wildwood Flower," were other dancing tunes.

We started in living rooms, usually at Aunt Margaret Lewis'. The furniture was pushed back; the band played in the hall. When she got a new barn, the dancing moved there. Later, we went to New Hope Campground where they had dancing in the dining room. Daddy loved dancing, even though he was a Baptist! Baptists thought dancing was a sin, as was drinking any kind of alcohol, even beer!

We also square danced at the White Cross Community Building. The community also had a shower for Sister Margaret and me when we got married weeks apart in September 1954.

Family Adventures

Flying

When we were young we had grand ideas like flying! If planes could do it, so could we. Brother Bob was chosen probably because he was the youngest and the smallest. We made his wings with newspaper and broom straw and tied them on him with tobacco twine! We were in the hayloft. One of us went to watch him fly and the others helped him get ready. Well. He jumped from the hayloft! We nearly killed him! No more inventions!

First Super Bowl

The first Super Bowl was played in January 1967. Mama Ruth was having the first Teer reunion at her house, so after lunch in the basement, the men watched the game in the living room on a little black and white TV – the first in our area.

Mouse in the house

My mother was scared to death of a mouse. Daddy always said, "would that man had the power over a woman that a mouse had." One time we were at Mama Ruth's. Brother Berry's wife Joanne, Bob and Berry came in the back door by the refrigerator. Mama and I had chased the mouse around under the cabinet and it had run up under the refrigerator just as brother Bob came in the back door. The mouse came out and ran up his pants leg. Berry grabbed his pants leg and held the mouse in Bob's pants. They hobbled out the door and turned the mouse loose. Bob was jumping up and down. We laughed so much. Joanne went into labor the next day with her first child, Donna.

Daddy

My daddy was diagnosed with brain cancer in 1958. I do not remember him ever complaining of headaches. He had been to feed the hogs behind the house near the pond. Lee was with him. He was 3 years old. Daddy walked in the door and fell down. He was having a seizure. We called the doctor (there was no rescue squad back then). Dr. Jones came in just as Daddy had another seizure and said, "He has a brain tumor." Walker's Funeral Home was our rescue squad. They took him to Memorial Hospital where he was operated on but they could not get it all.

He had the first seizure in February 1959, the second in May, then he had the surgery. The doctor – Duggor was his name – said he would live six, maybe nine months. He lived nine years! We credited it to prayer! The preacher, Caldwell Williams, had a prayer meeting at Antioch Church the night before. The church was full.

R.L.

This is a love story that ended way too soon.
R.L. (Robert Lee Lloyd) was born July 26, 1935. He was born at home (that's what Eleanor said). His daddy was Nevie Green Lloyd. His mother was Clara Lucy Lloyd. No kin to Mr. Green! Though, her mother's name was Nevie, also. Green was much older than Clara. She was his second wife. His first wife, Maude, died from a ruptured appendix when their son Dalton was 2. Green was 36 when he married Clara, who was 18. Their children were Everett, Leta, Peggy, Robert Lee and Eleanor. Eleanor was the only one not born at home. Clara bled so much that she nearly died in her other birthings so Doctor Lloyd (no relation) sent her to Duke Hospital when she went into labor.

From left are Dalton Lloyd, Everett Lloyd, Nevie Green Lloyd holding R.L. Lloyd, and Clara Lloyd.

Mr. Green said R.L. was the best child he had. He surely must have been because he quit school in the ninth grade to work cutting logs for a sawmill (which was run by Donald Branson) so he could raise his little sister, Eleanor, who was 9 years old. Their mother, Clara, was the bread winner. She had worked at Carrboro Cotton Mill. She died on December 15, 1951, of an allergic reaction to a sulfur drug. She had boils all over her body. She was 45. Mr. Green was a hard man who was known for his anger.

Earl Land was his first cousin. He said R.L. wanted a horse really bad. He put a bridle on a calf and rode it like a horse.

We went to the movies at Carolina Theater for our first date. I do not remember how long we dated, but I was in the 11th grade. We married on September 1, 1954. I was a senior in high school. We got married at Davis Street Methodist Church. His sister Peggy and my brother Berry were there. We went to Carolina Beach for a honeymoon.

We lived at Mr. Green's to take care of Eleanor, but he got mad at me for not having coffee for breakfast. We moved to Miss Betty Ward's. She had a three-room apartment.

I loved R.L. from the fifth grade. He was three years older than me and two grades ahead of me. I had skipped third grade. His first love was baseball. He played second base and was a strong hitter. He was on a semi-pro team which played local teams. It was the White Cross team. They played at White Cross, Orange Grove, Carrboro and Eli Whitney – always on Saturday afternoons. I went to all the games, even when I was nine months pregnant. Our son, Lee (Robert Lee, Jr.), was at a game weeks after he was born.

R.L. joined a semi-pro team from Roxboro. He was playing for them when he was killed. (September 10, 1959, in Roxboro)

Frances and R.L.

29

Lee's Birthday

Lee was my first born. He was born July 29, 1955. We had been married September 1, 1954. Back then, we didn't know what the child was going to be. We thought we were going to have a girl. Lee was three weeks late from the due date. He weighed 9 pounds and 9 ounces when he was born. I was in labor for three days. R.L. was thrilled to have a boy. We named him Robert Lee Jr. While I was in the hospital with Lee, R.L. and my brother Bob came to see me. At that time, the father did not stay at the hospital. After they stopped to visit, they went on to a square dance. Not wise! They made me so mad! We came home and stayed at my mother's house for a few weeks. Back then, you didn't get out of bed much as a new mother. We lived across the road from my mother. Lee had pneumonia when he was four or five months old. My sister had a baby girl, Anita, three months before Lee was born. We all lived close to Mama, so we were together every day – gardening, canning, freezing vegetables and tending to the babies. To this day, Lee and Anita are close. My sister Margaret had two more girls and a boy. I had Lee and Lisha. We had our own day care.

R.L. and Lee enjoying the beach

SEPT 1960

Lisha's Birthday

Lisha was born early on October 4, 1958. She was three weeks early. Lee was late by three weeks, so I was surprised when I woke up in labor. I thought I was dreaming I was in labor.

We were living in Frank Crawford's house on Hwy 54. Mrs. Lula, a neighbor, came in to fuss at R.L. because his dog was eating her chicken eggs. When she saw me having a contraction, she had a "fit"! She packed all that was in my underwear drawer and pushed us out the door. I was eating ham biscuits because I knew I would not be allowed to eat at the hospital.

MAY 1959

RL with Lisha and Lee. This is the only photo of Lisha with her father.

We gathered up Lee and took him to Mama Ruth's. We were still in no hurry. She, too, sent us out! With Lee, I was in labor over the course of three days and in hard labor 13 hours. No hurry! I needed a bra. We stopped in Carrboro at White Oaks Department Store. When the clerk saw me in labor, she too, sent me out the door!

When I got to the hospital, R.L. took me in the ER, and saw them take me away after he kissed me. He went home to watch the World Series at Mama Ruth's. Then, he went to White Cross Store, where Mama Ruth told them to tell R.L. he had a girl.

Lisha weighed only 6 pounds, compared to Lee's 9 pounds. She was 18 inches long. Lee was 21. I was going to name her Angela, but R.L. said, "no, she's Lisha Ruth." Mama Ruth and R.L. named her. R.L. was in love with her from the moment the nurse let him hold her hours after she was born.

The Day R.L. Died

For reasons unknown, Mama's house was getting a huge cleaning. The organdy curtains hung on the clothes line, starched to a crisp, yet to be ironed. The hardwood floors were cleaned by hand using Varsol. All was in upheaval. We don't clean like that today. In the midst of all this – I still remember that I was standing at the open front door – Mama says, "I wonder if we are cleaning for a funeral." Not so strange a question considering Daddy had major brain surgery for cancer a few years before and back then medical treatment was not what it is today. He was living under a cloud of grace. As we labored away, Mama and me, I opened the refrigerator for something saying as I did so, "I sure hope if anything happens to RL that I don't carry on like Aunt Thelma." She was still moaning over the death of a husband she seemed to hate all the while he was living – so that now her groanings seemed odd to me.

At that instant, the ring of the phone signaled my bridge falling! For years I had a recurring dream that I was in a car going across a bridge when it started falling. Daddy always came to comfort my cries in the night, always before the bridge hit bottom.

I heard the operator ask for Mrs. Andrews. No one ever asked for Daddy. I offered to take the call when I heard Arthur Dawson, RL's foreman at the sawmill say, "Operator, ask for Mrs. Andrews." He wouldn't talk to me. I knew as one knows that this was not good!

As Mama took the call, her body slid down the wall. Over and over she was saying, "oh no, oh no." Practically screaming, I said, "Mama, is he hurt?" Her reply a stunning, "no, baby, he's not hurt. He's dead."

Out the door I ran screaming to find my Daddy. He and Granddaddy were working on a fence. They rushed to meet me, holding me close, then slapping my face to stop the hysteria. I told them the awful news – my love since fifth grade, the father of my two babies was no longer alive. Dead. Gone. In a flash.

Daddy instantly said, "Your bridge just broke!" And, so it did.

R.L. tried to prepare me for this. Even when our baby girl was in the womb, he was concerned that he would not see her grow up. (A close friend had been killed in a car accident a few months earlier just after they had been by to tell us they were having a baby.) R.L. had a sawmill when he was killed. He was only 24 years old. He was cutting timber in Roxboro and staying in a boarding house over there. He was afraid he would be killed in a wreck driving back and forth. Did he have a premonition? I wonder.

He came home every Friday, but on Monday night he came home! He had just driven up that morning but he said, "I just wanted to be with you and the children."

When he left, he said, "I'll see you Friday one way or another." When he left that Tuesday morning, he said, "Goodbye." Never before had he done that. He always said, "So long." Goodbye was too final, he thought. I was upset by that as he drove away.

R. L. Lloyd

On Sunday before that fatal Wednesday, he also said he wanted me to marry again because he wanted his children to have a father. I promised with a joke, "Sure, I'll be dancing six weeks later."

Everyone loved and respected him.

Glenda Mauer said it was such a shock. Grown men cried when they heard about his death at Andrews Rigsbee Hardware in Carrboro and at Kirby's store out near our house on Hwy 54.

33

Joanne Andrews said Mama called her at work. Word spread all over in a few minutes. It was September 10, 1959, a Friday.

Precious Memories

September 10, 2016. On this day in 1959, my love died. I do not have to see a calendar to know. My heart tells me. Today is no different.

Brother Berry's birthday was the next day.

Notes I found that I had written in January 2012 and September 10, 2014:

"Five short years of marriage, a lifetime of memories."
"His life has never left me. Out of love, I write this."
"Our honeymoon at Carolina Beach. We went to Airlie Garden and walked among live 100-year-old oak trees, got donuts from Britts, bought me shell earrings and stayed at Farmer's Cottage."
R.L was killed by a falling tree at his sawmill site on a track of timber on Roxboro on September 10, 1959. Lee was 4 years old. Lisha was 11 months. She walked a few weeks after he died. He wanted to see her do that so badly.

September is a difficult month for me. R.L. and I got married September 1 (would be 62 years as I'm writing this in 2016). He was killed by a falling tree on September 10.

Lisha wanted to get married on that date, a Saturday, but Joel's family could not get here, so they got married on the 2nd, a Sunday.
After R.L.'s death, I knew I had to get some way to support my children and myself. They only got $250 per month for both of them. So, I tried to go to college at Elon College in Burlington, NC, (which is where Kristen and Caleb both went) – which was too soon after R.L.'s death. I remember sitting on the rock wall up there and crying. I never went back. Instead, I went to secretarial school in Chapel Hill the next fall for nine months. I even learned shorthand!

My first job was in the UNC Purchasing Department. I was the director's secretary. I left three years later to stay home with Lee and Lisha after I had married Billy McCoy.

I remarried less than two years after R.L.'s death (August 4, 1961), way too soon. I did not love Billy McCoy. I was afraid. I had two small children and had never worked. The marriage was doomed before it began. His daddy told me as we waited outside Antioch Church, "It is not too late to end this."

He knew and so did I, but the church was full and the candles were lit. The preacher waited.

Unknown to me, Billy had a drinking addiction. So did his father, Garland. I tried unsuccessfully to deliver him.

Finally, I could not live in that environment, so I started the leaving because of his alcohol problem. This was in 1973. We were married 12 years. Billy was good to me and my children. I learned a good lesson. You can't manage somebody else. If I hadn't married him, however, I wouldn't have met my restoration in Lester Howard.

Divorce

Finally, I left him for the third time. I took Lee and Lisha and went to Mama Ruth's. She told me that if I went back to Billy McCoy she would not allow me to take the children with me. No way was I going to give them up!

A few days later I went to see a lawyer in Siler City, Mr. Gunn. Billy got a lawyer in Pittsboro. Billy was in the house. Lee was driving from Mama Ruth's so he and Lisha could go to school in Pittsboro. She lived outside Chapel Hill.

When Mr. Gunn asked me what I wanted, I gave him a figure and said I wanted to get back in the house until Lee finished high school. Well, his lawyer told him to get out right away, and he did! He went next door to Aunt Kathryn and Uncle John's. I went back

35

home to our house.

I sold the house in 1974 and moved to a condo in Cary. Lisha went to Cary High School for a year. Lee was already graduated. He lived at the beach, working with a builder and being a beach bum. I told him that if he wanted to be a beach bum, he had better be the best on the beach.

Well! Not long after that, he came home (to Mama Ruth's where I had moved back to from Cary). He had long, straggly hair and a beard! He told me I was looking at a Navy diver. ("God help us if our nation has come to this.") I told him the recruiter would tell him anything to get him to sign up.

Lee made diver! No easy feat. He was mistakenly sent to California to Seal training school but he got those orders changed. He went to Pensacola, FL. He called me when he knew he made diving school and asked my permission to go forward. He said it was the second most dangerous profession in the world. Fireman was the worst!

I asked him if this was his dream. He said, "Yes." I told him to go for it!

As a Navy diver, he worked in Cuba at Guantanamo Base and at a base in Sardinia, Italy. Lee's diving career ended when he was on a barge that sank during a hurricane. There were over 200 on it. Nineteen were divers. The rest were Mexicans who spoke no English and could not swim.

Hair Styles in the 1960s

When I was married to Billy McCoy, I used to get my hair done every Friday. I never brushed it or combed it for a week. That was the style. To keep my hair in place, I would wrap it in toilet paper every night. We always said that my marriage didn't last because Billy didn't know which end was up when he came to bed at night. If you had told that I would have my hair cut short and that I would wash it and blow it dry every morning, I would never have believed it.

Near Death

In 1973 I had what was to be minor surgery, but something went wrong, and I started hemorrhaging in the recovery room. I tried to tell the nurses that I was wet all the way to my neck but they did not believe me. There were curtains between the beds. I was concerned about a little boy in the bed next to me. Finally, a nurse looked under the sheet and went into alert mode. By then I was unconscious or near death. Joanne Andrews had been sitting with me. The nurse told her to call in the family. I wanted to tell her I was fine. By then I was out of my body – and I was fine! But, no words came out. I thought I was near the ceiling and all was well. It was not!

I remember going down a tunnel toward a very bright light when voices were calling my name. "Mary Frances, wake up!" Then I came back! My life changed forever but not as much as being born again in 1980!

After My Divorce

After my divorce, I lived with my niece Anita in the little house in Calvender outside Carrboro. She had a next-door neighbor named Kenny Rogers and he was good looking. He was a Chapel Hill policeman. We decided that he needed to meet Anita's friend Raney, so we had her over one night, so we could introduce her to him. They hit it right off that night. They got married and she moved with him to the mountains. He bought a Christmas tree farm. She decided she would start painting because she was so isolated. Today she is a renowned artist. I have one of her originals in my home. I told her, "Raney, I want you to paint me a field of daisies. Daisies are special to me because when R.L. and I were first married and I was big and pregnant, we drove by a huge field of daisies on the way to his daddy's house. The field was between his daddy's house and Joe McCauley's Store. I asked R.L. as we drove by that field if he loved me. He looked at me and said, "as much daisies as in Joe's field." The field was covered in daisies. That was in June and Lee was born in July. When I married Lester, I wanted a picture to put on a big white wall in my house in Fuquay. I called Raney and asked her if she could paint me a picture of a field of daisies. She said that if I would wait until they were in bloom she would see about painting it. Kenny drove by that same field to buy nursery products. I asked her in January, so we waited until June. She called and said she started the picture. I told her that bluebirds were Lester's favorite bird and asked her to put one in it. She painted the picture with an obvious blue bird and one hidden in the daisies that represented my late husband R.L.

The Day the Snake Got in the Basement

(Frances wrote this when she was living at Mama Ruth's.)

Probably when a snake gets in a basement, it is not a real big thing. But, at our house, it is. There has not been a snake seen in the basement in the thirty years we lived in this house. There has not even one been seen in the yard except for a time or two. So, a snake in the basement was a new thing for us. Not that I was there to see it. I was at work. But, Tracy (my great-niece) and Candee (my niece and Tracy's aunt) were here. Candee was washing clothes in the basement and when she went down to check on them, Tracy stayed at the top of the stairs just to talk to Candee. You see, Tracy is at the age she is almost grown, 10 years old. So, she can tell it like it is, and she likes to be where she can tell it like it is a lot of the time.

Anyhow, Tracy noticed a movement near her play refrigerator, which had been moved to the basement – the last place before the dump. When she looked closer (as close as you can from the top of the stairs) she saw a great long snake, black. It moved, and very calmly she told her aunt Candee to be very careful when she came

38

around to the steps because there was a snake down there. Now, Aunt Candee had been around long enough to know that WE DON'T HAVE SNAKES IN THE BASEMENT. Sure enough, there was a snake between Candee and the steps. Well, somehow Candee got up the stairs. I'll probably never know how because Aunt Candee still gets rather excited about the whole thing. About this time, Donna, Tracy's mother, came in. They tried to call several other members of the family, me included. You, see, I live here with my mother, the grandmother to all these girls, and it is my job to know what to do in EVERY situation. But, I was not in my office, so they had to resort to other means to take care of the snake. Suddenly, they remembered that their Aunt Tammy's husband, Dale, was asleep upstairs. (Yes, this house has a basement and an upstairs.) Dale was asleep because he is a policeman and it is his turn to work all night, so he was trying to sleep during the day. Of course, I'm sure by this time Dale had figured out something must be going on – what with Tracy, Candee and Donna, not to mention Mama Ruth all excited about a snake in the basement. I forgot to mention that Hannah, Tammy and Dale's cocker spaniel was also in on the snake thing. She can get rather excited, even without a snake in the basement. I have an idea it was a bit rowdy.

Well, they go to get Dale up to kill the snake – and guess what? Dale is no snake lover either! But, he did go to the third step from the bottom and look at it, all coiled up, ready to strike. There was no hoe nearby, only a shovel, but Dale wanted an instrument which he could use, so he sent Donna out to fetch a hoe. In the midst of the confusion, Mama Ruth decided on a way to take care of the whole mess. "Just shut the door and leave it down there," she said. I suppose by now Mama Ruth had had it with three girls and a dog and a policeman all trying to get rid of a snake in the basement. By the time I got home, however, the snake had been killed and thrown out in the corn field, and everyone had settled down. Everyone that is except Tracy – she was still a bit excited at 8:00 tonight. As was Donna and Candee. Dale just went on to work.

More Snakes

We seemed to have a lot of problems with snakes! I have written about the snake in the basement of our new house, but prior to that we had a black snake in the attic of the old house! We kept hearing something up there, but we four children were too scared to go up there. Mama was not! She came down with it on a broom! I guess she killed it, or might have left it alive to eat rats, which she was terrified of. Daddy said, "oh that he had the power over a woman that a mouse had!"

The Beach

In 1988, I transferred from the School of Library Science to the Institute of Marine Science in Morehead City. I rented a condo over on the beach in Pine Knoll Shores.

That was a miracle! It was the first of June and condos were rented. I believed God would provide. I had told everyone that I was moving to the beach to meet my husband, so there would be a place for me.

When I walked into a rental agency, someone who owned one of the condos had just left and wanted a long-term rental! I got it! Also, when I decided I wanted to live at the beach, I was going to take early retirement to do so. When I told a co-worker – Gerry Compton – she said there was a position open at the Institute. When I called the Personnel Department, they said the opening for applications was that afternoon at 3 p.m. and they had 49 applicants! I rushed down with my papers. Well! They interviewed me and I got the job by God's grace.

Turned out that Lester would not have agreed to see me if I hadn't been at the beach. When Clinton and Joyce told him about me, they said, "She lives at the beach, so if you do not like her, she will not be here to bother you."

I loved living at the beach. I moved there in June of 1988, eight years after I had been Born Again.

I was praying as best I could when God gave me a vision. It was a prayer of repentance, "Lord, forgive me. I yield myself to you. If you have a husband for me, send him to me." I saw a man way off in the distance. He looked like Percy Howard. I knew it would be a while and it was eight years before I met Lester.

Born Again!

On May 10, 1980, I was Born Again to a life in Christ. After I divorced Billy McCoy, I was angry with God so I "left" Him to live in the world's ways for eight years! But, Jesus never left me!
God sent Gerry Compton to work for us in the School of Library Science. She did not have to work. She drove a Mercedes 50 miles each way to work, and wore a full-length Aigner leather coat! One day, I was complaining about a "no good" man I was involved with. Gerry looked at me and said, "why are you doing this to yourself?"
It was the look Jesus gave to Peter in the garden. That look changed my life forever! I now had a new love! My prayer was, "Lord, if you have a husband for me, please bring us together. I'm done looking!"

But, first I must tell this: I started going to a Bible study at lunch on Wednesdays. Fred Brooks, the chairman of the Department of Computer Science, started the study. He was the inventor of the main frame computer. In that study, I heard Lib Jones, Dr. Brooks' secretary, say, "You need the baptism in the Holy Spirit."

I had been taught in the Baptist Church that was of the Devil! But, I asked for that baptism and received it.

I began a new life! Old things passed away. Even the trees were greener, and Jesus was real to me. The Bible was understood. It was life to my body, peace to my soul and joy to my spirit!

41

Praying in tongues is a sign of the baptism in the Holy Spirit.

God placed a strong desire for that experience, whatever it was. I prayed for it on my knees, lying on my bed, on the floor, for days and days! Finally, I gave up one night when I went to bed.

"Lord, you know what I need. I give up! You can Baptize in your Holy Spirit when you want to!"

I was through begging. That night, I dreamed I was lifted up and into His Spirit. Jesus did baptize me!

(This was before I met Lester Howard. I was Born Again on May 10, 1980.)

How I Met Lester

Hand of God – Spur of the Moment

I moved to Pine Knoll Shores in June 1988 to work at the UNC Marine Institute. It was not long before Joyce and Clinton Copeland came down and while they were there they picked me up to take me out to eat. It was in the first few weeks of November. As I told them about being Born Again, they said I should be sharing my life with someone. "You owe me," I told them. I had introduced them to each other 20 years before. So, Clinton and Joyce began to think of someone. Lester Howard! His wife had died in May of cancer in 1988. They told me they would fix us up when they heard he was "stepping out."

Their daughter had had a baby. It was Thanksgiving, so I had come up from the beach to be with family. I was at Berry's and Joanne's. I was planning to stay at the beach but decided on the spur of the moment to be with family, so I went up to Berry's to spend the night. The decision to go back home in Chapel Hill changed my life! I called Clinton and Joyce to see if I could come by on Friday to see their new grandbaby on my way back to the beach. They said yes!

Well, later that day while I was at Berry's, Clinton called back and said they had a date for me for Friday night. I told them that I had no clothes except the jeans which I had on. Clinton said, "go shopping Friday!"

So, I went shopping with Joanne on Friday. I got a blouse, slip, skirt, sweater, shoes, pantyhose and earrings. I told Joanne that I felt like I was buying my wedding trousseau! Little did I know!

I had made a list of what I wanted in a husband, so God would know. On it was:
- He was a Christian
- He had loved his wife (if he had any)
- He loved his children (if he had any)
- He liked to travel and could afford to travel
- Had a sense of humor
- Was between 60-70 – he was retired
- Wore wingtips or loafers (no flipflops – no hippies, no tennis shoes)
- Size 10 ½ shoe (we decided that at work)

A complete description of Lester Howard!

He had sold his trucking company (18 wheelers which hauled bricks for Cherokee Brick Co.) (Navaho) Just before I called Clinton and Joyce, I had prayed, "Lord, if you have a husband for me, let me know. I just want to serve you." I crawled into bed to sleep. As my eyes closed, I saw a vision of a man's face. He looked like Lester's older brother, Percy. I said, "Lord, that is Percy Howard and he is married!" Lester was one of seven boys and they all look somewhat alike! Percy, Ray, Lester, Wilbur, Jerry, Dan and Calvin. God had given me a vision. Clinton and Joyce had me come to their house at 6 p.m. so we could visit for a few minutes. Lester came at 6:30. When they introduced us, they said, "you know Lester?" I said, "yes," though we had never spoken to each other! I had seen him in the vision. First thing I looked at, after his blue eyes, was his shoes.

He had on wingtips! I also had sung in the choir at Bell's Baptist Church for his mother's funeral and father's.

Clinton and Joyce took us to TGI Friday's on Oberland Road, Raleigh. Lester and I sat in the back seat, but he talked to Clinton all the way about Navaho Trucking Co., and Dan buying the company.
As we were eating, I asked Lester a question, to which he answered, "Yes, sir." I said to him, "I am a girl."

He said, "I know that," in what I thought was a very sexy voice. I was falling in love!

When we got back to Clinton and Joyce's house, they wanted to play cards. They went to the back of their house, leaving us alone in the kitchen. They had left a note pad and pen on the counter. Lester asked me for my phone number and wrote it down on a sheet of the pad.
As we were playing cards, I trumped his hand and he said if I did that again he would tear up the note as he patted his shirt pocket. I was touching his leg with mine. Sure enough, I had another chance to trump his hand and did! He said he knew I had spunk.

So, he called me the next week to see if he could come to see me. And he did.

When Lester called, I had two questions for him. "What size shoe do you wear?", and "Do you know how to walk in a chicken lot?" His answers were, shoe size 10 ½ and "very carefully!" He passed the tests!

He asked if he could come to see me and take me to his beach house in Surf City. I was very skeptical, but he assured me he was a gentleman. The house had a downstairs apartment where he would sleep. So, he picked me up in Pine Knoll Shores and away I went. When we got there, he had a box of candy on the counter. It was there, in the hall, where he kissed me for the first time!

44

Lester's nickname in high school was "Romancy." It suited him well, though he was shy.

At his beach house, he did sleep downstairs. The next morning when he came upstairs he said he nearly froze to death. There was no heat down there and it was very cold outside. So, the next night he slept in the other bedroom that was upstairs. I never slept, thinking he was just across from me and I am going to marry him! My much prayed for husband!

Getting Married

Lisha was pregnant with her first child, Kristen. I called Lester to tell him I was leaving to go to Clearwater, FL, after Lisha called to say she was in labor, three weeks early, January 26, 1989. I was going to drive down there, something I had done for five years. But, he said, "no," he would drive me. I went up to Cary, thinking we would leave as soon as I got there on Friday. To my great surprise, his girls had a party planned for Sharon, his youngest, for Friday night. Much to my dismay, we did not leave until Saturday morning. I was upset! He was torn between his girls and me. So, we left on the next day in his Lincoln Town Car. On the way, he said we are going to get married in Florida. I was in shock!

He said, "my girls are upset with me seeing you, so I will give them something to work with!"

We arrived in Clearwater. I was to stay with Lisha and Joel and the baby, Kristen. I do not remember, but I think I did not stay at Lisha's – to my deep regret. I stayed at a hotel in one of the rooms. Lester had rented two rooms. We stayed in separate rooms. Insane in retrospect! I should have stayed at Lisha's!

Then, he decided we would get married when we had been there two days. He asked Lisha what we had to do to get married in Florida. Lisha took us to the courthouse in Clearwater, where we got our license to marry. The clerk said if we came back after 2 p.m., she would marry us. I said, "no, I want Lisha's pastor to marry us."

Well, after we went to lunch Lester wanted to go back to the courthouse. I thought out loud, "why not?" so we did! It was January 30, 1989.

Lisha was our matron of honor. Kristen was our maid of honor at 4 days old! Then, we went back to their apartment. Oh, I should tell that we stopped at JC Penney and bought wedding rings. Lester had given me an emerald and diamond ring the third time I saw him. He said it was a sign of his intentions. When I went in to work at the institute of Marine Science and showed them my ring, one lady said, "you better brace yourself. He is going to marry you!"

Deliverance

I started smoking the day R.L. was killed. On the way to Roxboro, Uncle Jim Snipes gave me a cigarette, said it would help calm me down. I had a balm! So, over the next 30 years I smoked about a pack every other day. I always said I would stop when God restored what I lost in R.L.'s death.

My second husband Billy McCoy was a smoker, so I have to say he was not my restoration. But, Lester Howard was my restoration!
Joyce and Clinton told me I had to quit smoking or he would not want to court me. When I was going to Cary to go on to Florida to see my new granddaughter, I smoked my last cigarette! I had always said I would quit when God restored what I lost when R.L. died, and I did! Never wanted another one! I did chew tons of Juicy Fruit gum. Cannot stand it now!

Lester Teaching Golf

Lester taught himself to play golf at 50 years old. He was so excited when he married me because he thought I would play golf with him.

He bought me golf clubs and golf shoes and got me all ready to play. He took me down Hwy 55 South near Angier to a golf course to teach me how to play. He took his ball out and got out at the men's tee. He hit the ball way out of sight. Then he took me to the women's tee to teach me. He was trying to show me how to hold my hands on the club, where to put my butt, how to stand and where to put my thumb. I started laughing and I dropped the club. I said, "Lester, no man has told me what to do my whole life, now you're going to tell me where to put my thumb?"

He got me all fixed and I hit the ball four feet away. I never really got the hang of golf. I never lost a ball because I never hit it where I couldn't see it. Golf was not my thing.

Lester Howard's Story

Lester Howard lived a full life and often very exciting. He married Evelyn Windham from Merry Oakes, NC. They lived with her mother. She was reluctant to leave her mother.

Lester was drafted shortly after they married. He thought since his younger brother was drafted, he would not be. That is why he married. He said he would not have married her if he had known he was going to war.

Lester was born on September 18, 1921, in Chatham County, NC. He was the second of seven boys. Pity their mother! Her name was Lillian Seymour. His daddy was Troy Howard. He was hard (mean, I say) on Lillian and the boys. He was not known as a kind man. Lillian was.

Lester's father was a farmer. They raised tobacco. Lester said as soon as he finished high school he would never touch the stuff again and he didn't! He went to work for Swift and Company

47

delivering meat to places that sold meat. Then, he got drafted during World War II.

Lester was sent to Waterboro, SC, for basic training. He was put in the Army Air Corp based on his test scores. He was 21 years old, older than most of the draftees. He was trained to be an instrument specialist working on B-25 bombers. He loved airplanes and flying all the rest of his life! He was allowed to come home for one night before being shipped out to the Pacific Theater. He could not tell anyone where they were heading. He wrote to Evelyn every day! She did not keep the letters! He also sent his monthly pay check.

Lester was sent to New Guinea for three years. He lived in a tent in the jungle with very primitive conditions. He was an entrepreneur even then. He had clippers and scissors to cut hair and get paid. He sent the money home to Evelyn, who saved all of it which he used to buy the store. He also won a lot of money playing poker. It was sent home, too. Lester had dengue fever while in the jungle, so he was sent to Australia to a hospital.

He loved Australia, and I think he also loved his nurse there. But, he had married Evelyn three months before he was drafted, so he came home! Before he came home, he was on a troop carrier ship in the Gulf of Leyte, off the coast of the Philippines, when it was hit by a kamikaze plane (Japanese suicide bombers). He was sitting on a bench near the edge of the ship playing pinochle (a card game) when he heard the plane's rat-a-tat-tat.

Lester rolled off the bench into the trough where water ran off when the ship was washed off. His partner, who was new, did not move! Lester said he could see through him! It was horrific. Lester suffered only head wounds. He had metal in his skull all of his life. The dead were many – in the hundreds. Lester survived because a young boy who worked on the ship pulled him into a supply room.

The wounded were sent to a hospital on the coast of Australia but Lester did not stay. He made his way back to his base. When he got there, they were having a memorial service for the men killed in the kamikaze attack. He read his name on the list of dead posted on the tent. When he walked in, he broke up his own funeral!

Lester was good at breaking up funerals! He died during an ice storm in February 2003. We were with him at home. The church at Bells Baptist Church was packed with people outside. He was buried in Apex Cemetery beside Evelyn. At his graveside, we had an Honor Guard and a trumpet player who played "Taps". The Honor Guard held up the flag between the family and the casket. Lo and behold, the casket started sliding off the frame. Twice he broke up his own funeral!

After the war, he owned the country store that had belonged to his mother-in-law. He increased the inventory and sales tremendously. One day, P.D. Hinsley, who was a truck driver for Cherokee Brick Company, stopped for gas. He was upset with hauling bricks. Lester told him he would buy the truck for what was in the cash drawer of the store. He got the truck for $2500. So began his trucking business. He added more 18-wheelers until he had fifteen! He never had a secretary but did hire his brother Don to help him. He named his company Navaho. He had traveled across country by car and had seen a village of Indians on a reservation. They carried their possessions on slides pulled by horses.

Adventures with Lester

Adventures
I have walked on a glacier (in Alaska)
Slept in a rain forest (in Costa Rica)
Walked where Jesus walked (on a trip to Israel, in Jerusalem)
Baptized in the River Jordan (in Israel)
Floated in the Dead Sea (in Israel)
Stood on a volcano (in Hawaii)
And fell into a garbage can in my back yard

Frances and Lester shared many adventures.

Lester and I traveled to a lot of places by motor home to almost every state except North Dakota, the Northeast and California, Hawaii and Alaska. I had prayed for a husband who liked to travel, could afford to travel, was retired so he could travel. He was all of those. The second time I saw him I was still working and had to work four more years! He said, "I want to travel, have planned my whole life to do so." He said he would like to travel with me! My dream come true!

Lester said if I retired early, he would make it worth my doing so. So, I said, "yes," and we got married and hit the road!

In addition to motor home travel, we went on a tour to Alaska - a cruise for three days, then land for 10 days. It was my first and last cruise! I got very seasick.

Walked on a Glacier

Lester and I went on a Country Tours trip to Alaska. Country Tours was sponsored by the magazine, "Country." He tried not to go but he had already paid for the trip. He was afraid of strangers. Always was. Lester loved the trip to Alaska once we got there! He still would not mingle and did not want me to do so. I did, however, to some degree.

We traveled by bus all across Alaska, stopping to see Bald Eagles at the city dump in one of the big cities. In Glacier National Park we walked on a glacier! We were there in July but were told to expect cool temps. It was hot. Folks who lived there were shocked, as were we! There was no air conditioning or even fans. We left windows open. There were no mosquitos up there!

Hawaii, Costa Rico, Puerto Rico

We also went to Costa Rico on a Country Tours trip. We stayed on both sides, the mountain side and the beach side. We stayed in the jungle one night where we slept with open, no-screen windows, no air conditioning or fan. We walked on swing bridges over the jungle. We were served beans for every meal – red beans for breakfast, green beans for lunch and black beans for supper.

On our trip to Hawaii we stayed with my Uncle Gaston's wife for several nights in Honolulu. Doris was his third wife. She was Japanese. They married during World War II. Our country was at war with the Japanese! Anyhow, Lester loved Hawaii! We stayed on several of the islands. We went to the National Cemetery, called the Punch Bowl, where Uncle Gaston was buried. We also went to Kilauea Volcano, which has been erupting for a long time – at least since the early 1800s. After less than two weeks, Lester decided we needed to leave – right then! We had reservations to fly out several days later, so I got them changed to a Monday.

Plane Trouble

We got to the airport early, so we sat where we could see incoming planes. I was uneasy when I saw one engine spitting sparks. Lester assured me it was Ok. We were at the very back and I was upset

51

the plane had not been cleaned. In Honolulu, there were no extra planes, so we got on the plane despite my "warning". There was no problem during take-off, but I recalled a crash off the New England coast which had happened the day we landed in Honolulu, and my anxiety only got worse. I was on alert big time! We were airborne 25 minutes when I relaxed. The New England flight that had gone down did so after 25 minutes.

Well! Suddenly, a girl in the middle section crawled over her seat to show us something coming out of the engine on our side. We were sitting over the wing's engine. Lester said it was what we see in the sky behind a plane in the air – called contrails. It was not contrails! Suddenly, the pilot came on the intercom and said, "Ladies and gentlemen, we have to return to Honolulu. We have lost an engine." The plane had three – one on each wing and one the tail. I looked across the aisle to a huge black woman who had on a big wooden cross. I told her we would pray and bring down the plane safely. And so we did!

The pilot also said that we had to fly 45 minutes to jettison the fuel. That is what the girl saw coming out of the engines. The plane became very, very quiet! The crying babies stopped crying. No one made a sound. When the plane started to descend, I saw firetrucks and ambulances lining the runway. I said to Lester, "We are in deep dodo." He said, "no, baby, we were in deep dodo 45 minutes ago. We are Ok now!" That was only the beginning of a long, complicated journey home.

We landed safely back in Honolulu but had to stay on the plane for three hours with no food while the airline found busses and hotel rooms for all 300 of us. Then, we had to get our luggage and wait in line for room keys. It was 2 a.m. Tuesday when we got to lay down. We had to get up and go down to the lobby where we waited to go to the airport all day! Finally, the plane arrived and we boarded. We had to stop in San Francisco, California, for fuel. Then we flew to Chicago where we changed planes. Finally! We got home late Wednesday night. Whitted Road never looked so good.!

Lester and I went to Puerto Rico with his neighbors, Coy and Trillo. When Coy asked us to go in a week, Lester said we could not get ready in such a short time. His first wife, Evelyn, would have panicked, but I said, "let's go," and got us ready in a few days.

Selling the Beach House

Kay had pulled a fit when she found out Lee and Renee and Seph were coming from Louisiana on July 4, 1989, and we were going down to the beach house for July 4. Because of her fit, the very next week we went down to Surf City for Lester to put the house on the market. No one, including his daughters, told him what to do!

About a year later, he built a log house in the mountains.

Mountain House

I had always dreamed of having a log house. That dream was fulfilled when Lester decided to build one on Mt. Jefferson in West Jefferson. We often went there just to tour and eat at the Shatley Spring Restaurant. Folks came from far and wide to eat there. It was always packed full.

We drove past a log home sales office on the way to Shatley Springs. One day we stopped and talked to Marvin Wilcox, a "pure bred" mountain man. He told us that Bill Woody might sell us a lot on Mount Jefferson and Lester bought that day! Marvin gave us a book of log house plans. We were hooked!

Lester made a deal with Marvin. He paid him for overseeing the log house construction ($500) to keep it on track. We went up weekends. I loved it!

We "moved into" the log home. Although, I could not get Lester to stay more than a weekend, it became a true second home.

Lisha and Joel were frequent visitors. His daughters seldom came up. Carolyn came one time, as did Kay. Her husband was afraid to stay there. Sharon and her family came more often, like once a year.

One of our favorite things to do at the mountain house was go to Tweetsie Railway and ride the train. We once rented a canoe from Zaloos Canoes. You could rent one and go down the New River. We were going down the river to have a picnic. Joel and Kristin and I rented the canoe. Kristin hopped out and got up on the bank ok but I turned over the canoe. The picnic cooler went floating down the river with one of the oars. Joel managed to get the canoe turned back over. He left Kristin and me on the bank and went down river for the picnic basket and the missing oar. Lester and Lisha and Caleb weren't part of that adventure. They were still at the log cabin.

Lester and Alzheimer's

When Lester was about 75, he became very difficult to live with. We had built the house on Whitted Road as well as the house in the mountains. We had been married seven years. I tried to tell his daughters Carolyn, Kay and Sharon (his favorite) that something was wrong, but they would not listen. My theory is that if you admit that there is a problem, you have to help. They were not much help at first.

The onset of Alzheimer's changed our lives dramatically! At first, I was the only one (and Lee and Lisha) who was concerned. He appeared to be Ok. It was hard for him to decide what

Lester Howard

54

to wear. Daily decisions were hard. Also, his driving became dangerous. I got a letter from the doctor that he should not drive. He never saw it! We went to the DMV in Fuquay. He knew it was so he could renew his license, so he was very nervous. I showed the lady the letter from the doctor. She said, "what do I need to do?" I said, "give him a written test. He can't pass it." He tried so hard, but he could not do it. I asked for an ID card, so she had him sit for a photo.

The idea of his having an ID card which looked like a drivers' license was questionable. He went to the driver's side when we left the DMV. He was angry when I stood in the way. This happened several times. Finally, I went to the dealership where he traded cars every year. He had a Chrysler car and I had a Chrysler Town and Country van. The owner of the dealership and I decided that I would trade both vehicles and get one.

It took a while, but Lester forgot that he needed to drive. He did tell me how to drive. He was not from a generation where women drove. He would sit on the passenger side and tell me where to put on the brakes. He said, "Brake, dammit!" or "dammit Frances!" He gave me a new name!

Lester never forgot the memory of me or our children. His two younger daughters came regularly, but his oldest daughter, Carolyn, moved to Annapolis, MD. I was shocked! She did not come for Christmas. She claimed Paul had only one day off. Her father was on his death bed and she did not have time to come see him. He died six weeks later. She got there a few days before.

Lester died on February 13, 2003. The Alzheimer's was overrun by the dying. He was clearer then than he had been for several years! Strange. Lester died during an ice storm. All his girls and Lisha and Lee were there. Hospice was helping us, though they were not there that morning because of the storm. Lee had gone home to get a shower, and Carolyn was checking on Paul, who had stayed in the hotel. So, when he took his last breath, they were not there.

Because of the ice storm, it took the funeral home four hours to get to our house. We sat with his body for all of that time. Some drank coffee and stayed in the kitchen.

When we were at the funeral home, over 400 came to the visitation. The crowd at the funeral at Bells Baptist was overflowing. He was a well-respected man. During the graveside service, we had an honor guard from Fort Bragg play Taps and hold up the flag that had been on the casket. At that moment, the casket started shaking and sliding off the part that it sat on! Lester was going to heaven!

Lester is buried in the Apex Cemetery. He had already bought a marker which had his name and date of birth on it. I was spooked by that! He did this when his first wife died.

A New Grief

New sorrow came last night as this thing called "grief" bores into my being, washing over memories from earlier times and goes ever deeper into my spirit. Will no memory be spared? Framed pictures of two remain on dressers and shelves, as grief stands resolute, reminding me over and over that there were two in the pictures of my memory. One is now gone.
My prayer, my plea
Come Holy Spirit
Stand by me.
Fill the empty space, your comfort, your presence, now my companion. The void of his departure goes ever bigger...yet I hold onto the hope that even as time creates this void, so too, time will fill that void.
Proverbs 15:13...But by sorrow of the heart the spirit is broken.
July 6, 2003

Weddings

Joel and Lisha

Lisha went to visit Lee in Louisiana and they went out on the town with his friends. She met Joel, who was a deep-sea diver like her brother. She said he had the bluest eyes. It was love at first sight. I went to the airport to pick her up when it was time for her to come home and she wasn't there. She decided to stay in Louisiana a few more days because she met the cutest boy! They saw each other for about six months before they got engaged. They were married September 2, 1984.

Lisha and Joel got married at Antioch Baptist Church outside of Chapel Hill. Joel's family came from Chicago. It was a fun time. Joel's family got introduced to North Carolina farm life. Family members stayed with my friends and family. The rehearsal dinner was a pig picking at my sister's house. My family all brought food. The bridesmaids were Lisha's cousins. The groomsmen were Joel's relatives. I made the bridesmaids dresses and the flower girls dresses. I made the flower girl's dress in two days while I was working full time. One of Joel's nephews was a junior usher. He had never had barbecue before and he was nervous. During the ceremony, he got sick and threw up everywhere. It almost broke up the wedding.

The reception was held at a country house. The reception was a family affair. Lisha and Joel went on their honeymoon at Carolina Beach at the Golden Sands Hotel. Joel's parents stayed at the same hotel. They had never been to the Carolina beaches and they spent some time there after the wedding.

After a few days, they were packing up the wedding gifts to go home to Louisiana.

Lee and Renee's Wedding

Lee and Renee got married in Houma at her parents' home on May 27, 1985. Lee had to go right back to diving offshore, so they delayed their honeymoon. I don't know if they ever did go on a honeymoon. I was there for the wedding, along with Lisha and Joel. They were living in Louisiana at that time. It was a small ceremony with just the immediate family and a few of Lee's friends. It was a sweet wedding.

Candee's Wedding

A year after Lisha's wedding, my niece Candee got married at the same church, with the same people, and low and behold her junior usher fainted during the ceremony. Fortunately, there was a heart doctor, who jumped over two pews to get to the junior usher. The groomsmen and the doctor carried the boy behind the pulpit and out a side door where they revived him. This time the preacher was prepared. When the little boy passed out, he said, "let us pray."

Grandchildren

Pictured from left are Caleb, Elan, Kristen and Seph.

Seph

Robert Joseph Lloyd was born on November 25, 1985 in Houma, Louisiana. He was born by C-section. I do not remember why. He was good looking from day one.

I flew down there when Robert Joseph was 3 weeks old. I was so excited to have my first grandchild! He had the colic, probably from breast feeding. I stayed about a week. Lee was working offshore on a deep-sea job, but he was home when Seph (a nickname Renee gave him) was born. He was so proud of his baby son!

Kristen

Kristen was born on January 26, 1989. I wanted her to be named after me, so Joel named her Mary Kristen. I was hoping for Frances, but Mary had to do. Lester stole the thunder from Kristen's birth by deciding to get married four days later. We got married on January 30. Kristen was Lisha's little baby doll. She was our maid of honor at our wedding. She was probably the youngest maid of honor there ever was.

Elan

Seph was five years old when Elan was born. Elan was born on January 22, 1990, just 360 days after her cousin Kristen. She was a Louisiana girl, born in Houma, and lived there until she was in the sixth grade. That's when Lee stopped diving and they moved to North Carolina. I was so excited to have my grandchildren in North Carolina close to me. Elan was a beautiful baby with green eyes and an olive complexion. She's still beautiful.

Caleb

Lisha and Joel came to tell us they were going to have another baby, due September 9. They had moved from Clearwater, FL, back to Cary when Kristen was 6 months old. When they told us about having a baby on September 9, Lester said, "it will be born on my birthday, September 18!" This in February or March 1991, months before he was born!

Well, as time neared for the September 9 birth, Lester remained steadfast about the 18th. Lisha said she wouldn't last that long. Sure enough, time went by and no baby! Lisha and Kristen came to our house in MacGregor Downs every day. And no baby! His girls had his party on Sunday before the 18th. When we left Sharon's, Lester said, "All is set for the baby to be born on my birthday."

Well, Lisha and Kristen came over that morning and she said, "well, Papa, no baby today." To which he replied, "the day is not over."

Lisha took Kristen upstairs for a nap after lunch. She came down with a severe pain in her back. Lester said it is labor. Sharon had just had Andrew, so I called her. She agreed. But, when Lisha called Joel, he told her to call the doctor, who told Lisha to go to the hospital. Joel told her to wait until he got off work! We called him back and said, "get home now!" It was almost 3 p.m. He came by and got Lisha. They got to the hospital around 4:10 and Caleb was born four hours later. It was 8:18 p.m. and he weighed 8 lbs. 8 oz., born on the 18th, Lester's 70th birthday.

From the day Caleb was born, he and Lester had a special bond. Lester also was intrigued by Kristen. He would let her comb or brush what hair he had, and dress him up in scarves.

Elan visited

I used to take the grandchildren on special trips. One time, Elan came to visit from Louisiana. I took her, Kristen and Caleb to the beach. We rented a dune buggy from Calico Jack, who took us on a ride down the beach. I said, "ain't we having fun!" We had so much fun on that trip.

Life After Lester

Alzheimer's Caregivers Support Group

As I was grieving after Lester's death, I realized I was also grieving for RL and my failed marriage to Billy McCoy. I also was exhausted! It took months for me to gain my strength back. Caring for an Alzheimer's person is/was all consuming.

Laura Gaddis started an Alzheimer Caregivers Support Group at the Guardian Angel Thrift Store in Fuquay-Varina. She gave all proceeds to AlzNC, an agency that helps families. I started going there when I learned about it in about 2001. Laura was the facilitator. Her mother had Alzheimer's disease. It helped to hear how others were coping with their loved ones losing memory. After Lester died, I continued going to the support group, in the spring of 2003. About three months after his death, Laura Gaddis asked me to facilitate the group. I agreed with pleasure!
This became my life ministry. The group started with just a few of us, maybe 10. Over the years it grew so much that we moved to Windsor Point where we met in their activities room. I began sending out post cards as a reminder of the meeting. It evolved to sending a letter each month. That evolved into a letter with bits of information about Alzheimer's, books to read, etc. I called these letters instructional, inspirational and informative. I sent out at least 135 letters and most became emails. Not all were caregivers, but people who were interested in what we were doing. I did this until I had a stroke in late December 2015. The ministry stopped, and within a short time the "ministry" ended.

Over the 13 years, it would be safe to say that we probably touched hundreds of lives. Many became friends. One is still my best friend – Mary Giles. Another is Mrs. Beatrice Lee, who is a minister of the old-fashioned kind! It matters not that our skin color is different, our blood is red!

Strokes

In December 2015, I was very sick from a viral infection and was treated with steroids. When I was in the midst of the first stroke, Carol Hamilton, a neighbor, was here (one of God's "accidents"). Carol googled the symptoms and called 911. They took me to Rex Hospital in Raleigh, where I was seen immediately. I was there for three days, then sent to Universal in Fuquay – not a good experience!

In January or February 2016, I had a second stroke which left my right side affected, so I practiced writing with this life story.

Death

Monday, July 17, 2017
My only sister Margaret died suddenly last week. She got very sick and was diagnosed with cancer of the pancreas just two weeks before she died. I am in shock!

Margaret's funeral was sweet. Gayle Andrews read a piece she had written about Easter egg hunts at Aunt Margaret's and Christmas family gatherings in the "Shed" with the "red neck" fire barrel.

Frances, Bob, Margaret and Berry

Recipes

Nana's Fried Chicken

One fryer, cut into pieces, or if you wish – just legs or breasts
Soak overnight (after washing) in buttermilk – covered
Remove from buttermilk and batter in House Autry Hush Puppy mix.
Squeeze gently to get mix to stay on chicken.
Heat Crisco (not liquid) in electric frying pan at about 425 degrees
(a drop of water dropped in the melted Crisco should bounce)
Place fattest part of the legs in center, then the rest of the chicken
goes in. Do Not pack it! No pieces should touch. You will probably
need to do several batches.
Watch carefully, turning to brown all sides. Cook about 20-30
minutes covered after browned. Drain on brown paper.

Making Mints

We made homemade mints for weddings and parties. We had a
little business. Mama Ruth, Berry's wife Joanne and I made mints
for showers and parties. We had a recipe that was a family
heirloom. They were the kinds that you would put in your mouth and
they would just melt. The last time we made mints together was for
Candee's wedding. Usually we just made them for Christmas.

Made in the USA
Middletown, DE
22 December 2019